Table of Contents

INTRODUCTION 3

INSTANT POT TIPS AND TRICKS 5

CHAPTER ONE: PALEO BREAKFAST IN INSTANT POT 7

    Magnificent Zucchini Breakfast 8

    Gentle Chia Pudding 10

    Hearty Carrot Breakfast 12

    Paleo Pancakes with Blueberries 14

    Strawberries Breakfast 17

    Breakfast Porridge 19

PALEO LUNCHES IN INSTANT POT 21

    Zuppa Toscana with Cauliflower 22

    Chunky Beef Chili 25

    Mexican Paleo Soup 28

    Creamy Squash and Apple Soup 31

    Paleo Pork Chili 34

    Turmeric Veggie Soup 37

PALEO DINNERS IN INSTANT POT 39

    Chicken Wings 40

    Italian Meatballs and Sauce 43

    Pork Chops 46

    Curried Coconut Chicken 48

    Salsa Verde Chicken 51

    Instant Coconut Quinoa 53

    Instant Pot Yummy Ribs 55

    Creamy Sweet Potato Mash 58

- PALEO SNACKS IN INSTANT POT 60
  - Caramelized Carrots 61
  - Sweet Potato Snack 63
  - Baked Apples with A Twist 65
  - Bread Pudding 67
  - Homemade Applesauce 70
- PALEO DESSERTS IN INSTANT POT 72
  - Paleo Avocado Chocolate Cake 73
  - Chocolate Fondue 75
  - Tapioca Pudding 77
  - Blueberry Mug Cake 79
  - Apple Chutney 81
- Paleo Diet Food List 83
  - Foods Not Allowed on The Paleo Diet 85
- CONCLUSION 86

INTRODUCTION

There are tons of diets out there that so many people are willing to try, in a bid to eat right. Well, the paleo diet is one of these diets. If you haven't heard of this diet yet, it's basically eating natural food. There is a mantra that goes 'if a caveman didn't eat it, why should you?'. The diet has been around for over 10,000 years. In a nutshell, paleo involves eating non-processed foods, just like our mother nature intended.

There are many reasons why you should consider going paleo. To begin with, you'd be ditching all the processed foods and going for more natural ones, which have less additives and sugar. This has a positive boost not only on your health, and weight but also on your energy levels. Our bodies weren't meant to handle large amounts of salt, sugar and grains. The best part? With paleo diet, you are no longer focusing on just how many calories you consume, but you work on eating right.

In addition, turning to paleo diet, you would mostly be required to eat more vegetables, fresh fruit, nuts, eggs, seafood and meat. For the fruits, opt for less sugary ones, with berries being the best option. You can eat nuts in moderation, but leave peanuts out of your meal plan. Use coconut oil for your cooking and olive oil or avocado oil for salads. When it comes to meats, always go for the lean cuts grass fed versions; veal, lamb, chicken, venison. Grass fed butter is also acceptable since it has a high nutritional value.

Avoid grains and legumes at all costs. There are some paleo dieters who don't mind including whole milk and fermented dairy products in their meals, but it's not entirely advocated. If you can, leave out milk and products such as ice-cream completely. However, you can use coconut milk for baking purposes.

There is always a grey area when it comes to knowing what paleo is and what isn't. Just like with any other diet, I recommend doing extensive research before starting out on the diet. This will help you know what you need to include in your diet, and what to cut off completely, and if this particular diet is suitable for you in general.

INSTANT POT TIPS AND TRICKS

The Instant Pot is gradually taking over the cooking world - and with good reason. This is one pot that allows preparing any food you have in mind, from baked foods to soups, salads and desserts, in just a few minutes.

Moreover, when using an Instant Pot, you don't need to linger in the kitchen stirring the food or monitoring the progress. Once you close the lid and seal the vale for pressure, you can go about your business until the beeper goes off. Did you know that you could also sauté using your pot? Quite fascinating, right?

If you are a beginner, or you'd like to buy an instant pot, here are a few things worth noting.

To begin with, always read the manual after you purchase your IP. This will allow you know the functions available and how to operate the pot. Do not forget to clean your pot thoroughly after each use to avoid contaminating your food.

In addition to this, always keep in mind that some foods may take longer to cook than the recipes call for, meats especially. Your instant pot will get super-hot while cooking, so it's advisable to be very careful especially when taking off the lid. Use oven mitts to avoid burning your hands as you handle the pot. Unless a recipe specifies to use a different button, always opt for the manual button.

You must be wondering why some foods require a natural release of pressure while some need a quick release. I recommend using a quick release for seafood or vegetables, basically foods that don't require lots of cooking time. A natural release is ideal for foods with lots of liquids or starch.

There are some of the tips you will need when using your instant pot. There are so many other hacks out there, and you can still conduct your research to learn more.

In this cookbook, I have compiled a list of 30 recipes, to begin your paleo diet with, and you can use your instant pot to make all the recipes. I used simple ingredients that are readily available, and ensured there were a few recipes for each category, ranging from breakfast, lunch, dinner and dessert.

CHAPTER ONE: PALEO BREAKFAST IN INSTANT POT

Breakfast is the most important meal of the day, as it helps you start your day on a high note. Ever tried going about your daily routine while hungry? This even takes a toll on your overall productivity.

Paleo breakfasts could seem quite simple, yet you can keep tweaking them according to your personal choices, within the diet foods. You can try out these 6 recipes and keep rotating them, depending on what you liked best, trying out the eggs, oatmeal and sweet potatoes and you won't regret it.

Magnificent Zucchini Breakfast

Eating a big chunk of veggies for breakfast may not sound as appealing, but it's something worth trying. I opted for zucchini because of its mild sweet flavor, and the fact that it doesn't take long to cook. The last thing you want is spending so much time cooking in the morning. The rest of the ingredients bring in loads of flavor and nutrition that you cannot afford to miss out on.

Total time: 15 minutes

Serves: 6

Ingredients:

- yellow onion, chopped - 1½ cups
- Mushrooms, chopped - 12 oz.
- Canned tomatoes, crushed - 15 oz.

- olive oil- 1 tablespoon
- zucchinis, sliced-8 cups
- garlic cloves -2 cloves
- basil spring, chopped - 1
- sea salt and black pepper to taste

Directions:

- start by adding your olive oil to your instant pot and use the sauté function to heat
- stir in the onions and garlic and allow to cook until fragrant, for about 2 minutes
- add the mushrooms and basil and season with salt and pepper
- allow to cook for an extra minute
- stir in your zucchini and tomatoes
- Close the lid and let the veggies cook for about 2 minutes on high pressure.
- Release the pressure naturally.
- Serve and enjoy!

Nutritional information: calories 180, fat 2, fiber 3, carbs 5, protein 6

Gentle Chia Pudding

Chia seeds have gained so much popularity nowadays, and for a good reason. They are wholesome and nutritious, and you can incorporate them in a million breakfast dishes. This is an easy to make, vegan and gluten free breakfast pudding that will fill you up all morning. The best part? You can make your pudding overnight, which gives you ample time to run your other morning routines easily.

Total time: 10 minutes

Serves: 4

Ingredients:

- chia seeds - ½ cup
- almond milk - 2 cups
- almonds - ¼ cup
- coconut, shredded - ¼ cup
- agave syrup - 2 teaspoons

Directions:

- add your chia seeds to the bottom of your instant pot
- top with the remaining ingredients, except for the agave
- stir to incorporate all the ingredients and cover your pot
- Select Manual cooking mode and set the timer for 3 minutes on high pressure.
- Once done, allow for quick release of pressure then serve, each bowl topped with a ½ teaspoon of agave syrup and some nuts and berries. Enjoy!

Nutritional information: calories 130, fat 1, fiber 4, carbs 2, protein 14

Hearty Carrot Breakfast

Ever imagined that you would have carrots for breakfast and end up liking it? This carrot breakfast dish is super easy to make, wholesome and insanely tasty. Carrots are naturally sweet so if you are not a fan of too much sugar, just skip out on the agave nectar. You will love that this breakfast dish is not only packed with protein, but it has loads of flavor that will help you kick start each day with so much zeal.

Total time: 16 minutes

Serves: 3

Ingredients:

- coconut milk - 2 cups
- raisins, ½ cup
- flax meal - 3 tablespoons
- carrots, chopped- 1 cup
- agave nectar- 2 tablespoons
- cardamom, ground- 1 teaspoon
- A pinch of saffron
- Some chopped pistachios or other paleo-friendly nuts for serving

Directions:

- Add your coconut milk to the bottom of your instant pot
- Stir in the remaining ingredients in the pot
- Secure
- Select Manual cooking mode and set the timer to 6 minutes on high pressure.
- Release the pressure and open the pot after that.
- Serve into breakfast bowls, topped with your chopped pistachios. Enjoy!

Nutritional information: calories 160, fat 2, fiber 2, carbs 4, protein 5

Paleo Pancakes with Blueberries

Fancy some homemade pancakes for breakfast? You can still make your pancakes in an instant pot and achieve the same fluffy and delicious result you get from a stovetop. If you opt to use more batter for each mold, remember to also increase the cooking time to ensure your pancakes are well cooked.

Not a fan of blueberries? You can leave them out or use your favorite fruits or toppings like raspberries or bananas. Add a few more tablespoons of maple syrup to give your pancakes that nice maple flavor. If your instant pot lacks the cake setting, simply use the pressure cooking function on high.

Cook time: 10 minutes

Serves: 2

Ingredients:

- coconut flour – 1 cup
- blueberries, well rinsed – 1 cup
- organic sweetener of your choice – ½ tablespoon
- egg – 1
- milk, coconut – ¾ cup
- melted organic butter, cooled – 1 tablespoon
- baking powder – 1 teaspoon
- maple syrup – 2 tablespoons
- sea salt – 1/8 teaspoon
- water – 1 ½ cups

Method:

- combine the flour, baking powder, salt and sweetener in a large mixing bowl
- in a separate small bowl, beat your egg
- stir in the milk, syrup and cooled butter
- pour your wet mixture into the dry mixture and mix gently
- fold in your blueberries
- divide your mixture equally into your silicone tray, each mold about ¾ full
- cover your tray with a paper towel followed by a cooking foil, ensuring to tightly wrap around the edges

- pour the water into your instant pot and place the trivet at the bottom
- place your silicone tray on the trivet and close the pot's lid
- press the cake function and set timer for 5 minutes
- allow for natural release then quick release after 3 minutes
- remove your tray from the pot and turn out flat on a surface to allow for easy removal
- serve topped with blueberries or any other topping of your choice and enjoy.

Nutritional Information: calories 375, fat 4, fiber 3, carbs 5, protein 7

Strawberries Breakfast

It's about time you ditched the conventional eggs or protein shakes for breakfast. How about you try this light and yummy strawberry breakfast? You will be amazed at how easy it is to make, strawberries are nutritious and sweet, which makes the whole dish super delicious. What's more? This is a gluten-free, dairy-free and grain-free breakfast that you can enjoy as a family.

Total time: 20 minutes

Servings: 2

Ingredients:

- flax meal - 3 tablespoons
- strawberries, dried - 2 tablespoon
- Water - 2 cups
- almond milk - 2/3 cup
- honey - ½ teaspoon
- sea salt to taste

Directions:

- add all your ingredients to your instant pot
- stir to combine well and cover the lid
- Select Porridge mode and allow to for 10 minutes.
- Let the Instant Pot release the pressure naturally then open the lid
- Divide between the plates, garnish with nuts or berries and enjoy!

Nutritional information: calories 150, fat 5, fiber 3, carbs 6, protein 8

Breakfast Porridge

If you are used to having grains or cereals for breakfast this porridge can be your go-to recipe when switching to Paleo. You will love how quick and easy this porridge comes together. It's insanely tasty and overly filling; you'll not be looking for snacks before lunch. There are so many ways you could enjoy your porridge; with a dash of cinnamon and maple syrup, a topping of fresh berries or apples. You can make your porridge in a large batch and reheat it for breakfast, with different toppings every day.

Cook time: 10 minutes

Serves: 2

Ingredients:

- Raw cashews, unsalted – ½ cup

- Pecans, halved – ½ cup
- Pepitas, shelled – ¼ cup
- Dried coconut shred, unsweetened – ½ cup
- Water – 1 cup
- Coconut oil, melted – 2 teaspoons
- Maple syrup - 1 teaspoon

Method:

- Start by combining all your dry ingredients and adding to a blender or food processor
- Pulse on high for about 30 seconds or until you get a meal-like mixture
- Gradually transfer your mixture into your instant pot
- Pour in the wet ingredients
- Close the pot and seal the valve
- Select 'Porridge' cooking mode, or cook on 'manual' for 6 minutes.
- Once ready, allow for quick release of pressure and uncover the pot
- Stir your porridge and serve with your favorite toppings. Enjoy!

Nutritional Information: Calories 230, Fat 13, Fiber 4, Carbs 15, Protein 6

PALEO LUNCHES IN INSTANT POT

If you haven't realized, the paleo diet calls for light meals. For your lunch, you can enjoy these delicious soups or salads. Having a light lunch is ideal because filling up on food can leave you feeling a bit overwhelmed and even sleepy. Feel free to substitute some of the ingredients I have used with your favorite ones, as long as they are allowed within the paleo diet.

Zuppa Toscana with Cauliflower

We all have those days we want to impress our family or friends with our culinary skills over lunch. This is one of those easy exotic meals you can prepare for a light lunch. It is super creamy and paleo and just the perfect blend between a soup and a salad. With about 6 net carbs in each serving, everyone will be asking for seconds.

Cook time: 45 minutes

Serves: 8

Ingredients:

- Ghee – 1 teaspoon
- Italian sausage, ground – 1 lb.
- Chicken broth – 6 cups
- Cauliflower florets- 3 ½ cups
- Italian seasoning – 1 teaspoon
- Garlic powder – 1 teaspoon
- Red pepper flakes – 1 teaspoon
- Fresh kale, roughly chopped – 5 oz.
- Coconut milk, full fat – 14.5 oz.
- Salt and pepper to taste

Method:

- Set the Instant Pot to High and add your ghee, allowing it to melt
- Stir in your ground sausage, select Manual mode and set timer to 7 minutes to allow the sausage to fully brown
- Add the broth, cauliflower, seasonings and red pepper flakes and keep stirring
- Allow the mixture to come to a boil then set the timer to 10 minutes
- Close the IP and let the contents simmer
- Once the time is up, stir in the kale and coconut milk and allow the soup to heat for another 5 minutes

- Season with salt and pepper
- Serve and enjoy

Nutritional information: calories 184, fat 3, fiber 3, carbs 6, protein 8

Chunky Beef Chili

I hardly want to leave out beans when making chili, but most paleo recipes will leave them out. The chili comes out just as amazing in a slow cooker, but it's an instant pot that really brings out the flavors and the wholesome taste. To give your chili an extra bulk, use tons of peppers and mushrooms.

Cook time: 1 hour 15 mins

Serves: 6

Ingredients:

- Beef chunk roast, cut into big cubes – 2 lbs.
- Oil, coconut – 1 tablespoon
- Chili powder – 1 tablespoon
- Cumin, ground – 2 tablespoons

- Paprika – 1 tablespoon
- Beef broth – 1 cup
- Mushrooms, baby Portobello – 8 oz.
- Onion powder – 1 tablespoon
- Green pepper, chopped – 1
- Tomato paste – 6 oz.
- Sweet bell peppers, chopped – 1 cup
- Garlic, crushed – 1 cup
- Tomatoes, crushed – 28 oz.

Method:

- Select the 'sauté' cooking mode in your instant pot, and adjust the heat to high
- Add your oil to the pot and allow to heat up
- Carefully add your beef chunks into the oil and allow browning on both sides
- Add beef broth and secure the lid
- Turn the IP's quick pressure release button ON to create pressure and use the Manual cooking mode, setting the timer to 20 minutes
- Once done, allow for quick release of pressure
- Uncover the pot and add the remaining ingredients
- Mix to combine well and secure the lid
- Select 'manual' mode and set timer for 5 minutes
- When time is up, allow for natural release of pressure

- Serve and enjoy with a gluten-free tortilla.

Nutritional information: calories 261, fat 4, fiber 3, carbs 8, protein 18

Mexican Paleo Soup

If you are a fan of exotic soups, you will definitely enjoy preparing this Mexican soup using your instant pot. It's so quick and easy to make, and it tastes great. To make this recipe fully paleo, I left black beans and corn out.

Cook time: 1 hour 15 minutes

Serves: 8

Ingredients:

- Chicken, whole – 1
- Sweet potatoes, well rinsed – 2
- Tomatoes, cherry – 1 pint
- Bell peppers, red – 2
- Fresh Cilantro, chopped – ½ cup
- Large onion, chopped – 1
- Garlic powder – 1 tablespoon
- Curry powder – 1 tablespoon
- Red pepper, crushed – 1 tablespoon
- Onion salt – 1 tablespoon
- Diced avocados to garnish

Method:

- Start by boiling your chicken for about 30-40 minutes
- Season with garlic and cilantro to taste
- Meanwhile, rinse your vegetables and dice them
- Sauté your onion and bell peppers in a small saucepan
- When the chicken is tender, remove from the pan and add your sweet potatoes
- Allow them to boil until tender. This takes about 15 minutes
- Use a fork to shred the chicken and add the chicken into the instant pot together with the broth, vegetables and spices

- Secure the lid and, select 'Manual' cooking mode setting the timer to 20 minutes
- Allow for quick release once done and serve your soup garnished with some diced avocados. Enjoy!

Nutritional information: calories 210, protein 14, fat 3, fiber 4, carbs 7,

Creamy Squash and Apple Soup

There is always one thing you can count on during those crazy cold winter days- soup! A tasty bowl of soup is enough to make even the chilliest day look bearable. This butternut squash and apple soup is creamy and delicious, and is bound to give you all the comfort in the world. Making this soup in an instant pot makes matters so much easier. You can enjoy your soup as a stand-alone when opting for a light lunch, or as a side dish paired with a healthy salad.

Cook time: 30 minutes

Serves: 10

Ingredients:

- Coconut oil – 2 tablespoons
- Medium sweet onion, chopped – 1
- Garlic cloves, minced – 3

- Medium butternut squash, peeled, seeded and sliced into 2 inch cubes – 1
- Medium sweet potato, peeled and cut into 2 inch cubes – 1
- Tart-sweet apple, cored and cut into 2 inch cubes – 1
- Sage, dried – 1 teaspoon
- Pumpkin pie spice – ¼ teaspoon
- Ginger, dried – ¼ teaspoon
- Salt, kosher – ½ teaspoon
- Cracked pepper, fresh – 1/8 teaspoon
- Stock, vegetable – 2 cups
- Coconut milk, full fat – ½ can

Method:

- Set your IP to 'Sauté' mode and add the coconut oil
- Once melted, add the onion and garlic and keep stirring for about 3-5 minutes or until fragrant
- Stir in the squash and sweet potato cubes and allow to cook for a few minutes
- Press on the cancel button and add the remaining ingredients, except coconut milk
- Stir and secure the lid, ensuring you sealed the valve
- Using the Manual mode, set timer to 10 minutes under high pressure

- Once done, allow for natural release of pressure then remove the lid
- Transfer your soup to a food processor or blender and pulse until smooth
- Add the coconut milk and any desired seasonings and blend once more to fully combine all ingredients
- Top with your favorite toppings and serve. Enjoy!

Nutritional information: calories 113, fat 1, fiber 3, carbs 6, protein 6

Paleo Pork Chili

This is an amazing lunch that you can prepare in your instant pot and have it on your table in just under 30 minutes. This paleo pork roll is packed with tons of flavors and is quite filling, making it ideal for lunch. The dish also reheats well, therefore you can enjoy it for breakfast the next morning.

Cook time: 30 minutes

Serves: 4

Ingredients:

- Sesame oil – 2 teaspoons
- Garlic cloves, minced – 3
- Onion, diced – ½ cup
- Green onions, sliced on bias – 5
- Pork, ground – 1 lb.
- Ginger, ground – ½ teaspoon
- Garlic chili sauce – 1 teaspoon
- Coleslaw – 14 oz.
- Coconut aminos – 3 teaspoons
- Vinegar, rice wine – 1 teaspoon
- Sesame seeds, toasted – 2 teaspoons
- Sea salt and black pepper to taste

Method:

- Turn your Instant Pot on High and heat the sesame oil
- Add the onion, garlic and white stalks of green onions
- Select the Sauté mode and allow this to cook until fragrant
- Stir in the pork, pepper, ginger, chili sauce and salt and allow to sauté until pork is fully cooked through
- Add the remaining ingredients and cook for a few minutes until the coleslaw is tender

- Turn off your instant pot and serve topped with green onions and toasted sesame seeds on a plate of lettuce leaves. Enjoy!

Nutritional information: calories 244, fat 8, fiber 1, carbs 7, protein 22

Turmeric Veggie Soup

Looking for a paleo cleansing soup recipe? How about you start with this turmeric veggie soup, which has loads of cleansing ingredients that can help with a much needed detox? You will love that this is a fragrant and super nutritious soup, delicious and very easy to make using your instant pot.

Cook time: 20 minutes

Serves: 6

Ingredients:

- Butternut squash, cubed – 4 cups
- Carrots, peeled and cut into chunks – 2 cups
- Large sweet potato, peeled and cubed – 1
- Medium onion, chopped – 1

- Garlic, minced – 2 tablespoons
- Fresh ginger, grated – 1 teaspoon
- Turmeric powder – 2 teaspoons
- Garam masala – 1 teaspoon
- Curry powder, milk – 1 teaspoon
- Cayenne pepper – ¼ teaspoon
- Sea salt – 1 teaspoon
- Vegetable broth, low sodium – 3 ½ cups
- Coconut milk, full fat – 14 oz.
- Coconut oil – 1 tablespoon

Method:

- Add all your ingredients to an instant pot and stir well
- Secure the lid and select the 'Manual' cooking mode, setting the timer to 20 minutes
- Once the timer goes off, allow for a natural or quick release of pressure
- Use an immersion blender to puree your soup or transfer contents to a food processor or blender and pulse on high until smooth
- Serve and enjoy

Nutritional information: calories 84, fat 2, fiber 3, carbs 8, protein 9

PALEO DINNERS IN INSTANT POT

Dinner is one of those meals that no one should miss, simply because a nice dinner goes a long way in helping you end your day on a high note. For the paleo dinner recipes, I went for those that won't take you too long to make. This is because most days, we are too tired to prepare dinner.

You will notice that there are mostly meat recipes in this category. To make your dinner more filling and wholesome, you can include your favorite fresh veggies. Keep in mind that meat may take longer than expected to cook well, therefore, you should take caution not to eat undercooked meat. Feel free to add more time.

Chicken Wings

Fancy some wings for dinner? We all have those days when all we want are some wings after a long day at work. Chicken wings take more than an hour to make, especially if you are marinating, and no one has time for that. With an instant pot, you can make savory low-carb, gluten-free and paleo wings in under 30 minutes, just by putting all your ingredients in the pot. You can always marinate your wings in the fridge overnight for more flavor.

Cook time: 27 minutes

Serves: 60

Ingredients:

- Chicken wings – 5 lb.
- hot sauce – 1 cup

- apple cider vinegar – ¼ cup
- cayenne pepper – 1 tablespoon
- ghee – 1 tablespoon
- black pepper – 1 tablespoon
- salt, sea – 1 tablespoon

For the coating:

- hot sauce – ½ cup
- ghee – 3 tablespoons

Method:

- start by mixing the hot sauce, vinegar, peppers, ghee and sea salt in a medium bowl
- set aside ¼ of the sauce for coating later on
- gently separate the flats of the wings
- add your wings and sauce to the liner pot of your instant pot and mix well
- close the Instant Pot, select Manual cooking mode and set the manual timer to 10 minutes
- open the lid of your instant pot when the timer goes off, making sure that the wings form a single layer in the pot.
- use your reserved sauce to baste the wings
- Set the manual timer on the IP to 5 more minutes and broil the wings uncovered.

- once your chicken wings are fully browned, coat them well in the sauce
- Serve while hot with your favorite veggies. Enjoy!

Nutritional information: calories 182, fat 4, fiber 2, carbs 6, protein 15

Italian Meatballs and Sauce

The best thing about meatballs is that you can pair them with just about anything. This makes this dish a dinner favorite in many homes. Try out these low carb, overly juicy and tender meatballs, keto and paleo friendly. Moreover, you get to cut down on time since the instant pot has a sauté feature, which leaves out the tasking sautéing in pan step.

Cook time: 10 minutes

Serves: 5

Ingredients:

- Beef, ground – 1.5 lbs.
- Olive oil – 1 teaspoon
- Marinara sauce, sugar free - 3 cups
- Fresh parsley, chopped – 2 tablespoons

- Parmesan cheese, grated – ¾ cups
- Flour, almond – ½ cup
- Eggs – 2
- Salt, kosher – 1 teaspoon
- Black pepper, freshly ground – ¼ teaspoon
- Garlic powder – ¼ teaspoon
- Onion flakes, dried -1 teaspoon
- Oregano, dried – ¼ teaspoon
- Water, warm – 1/3 cup

Method:

- Add all your ingredients apart from the sauce and olive oil in a large mixing bowl
- Mix well to incorporate all the ingredients and form about 15 2 inch meatballs
- coat the bottom of your instant pot with your olive oil
- Gently place your meatballs in the pot, 0.5 inches apart. Do not press down
- Select the Sauté mode to brown both sides well
- drizzle the marinara sauce on the browned meatballs to coat them
- close the lid of the instant pot and set it to manual mode
- select the low pressure function and set the time to 10 minutes

- once the time is up, allow the pot release the pressure and open the lid
- serve your meatballs with a side dish of your choice and enjoy

Nutritional information: calories 130, fat 3, fiber 2, carbs 6, protein 6

Pork Chops

If you love pork, this is a quick and easy paleo pork chops recipe that will leave you asking for more. For a more complete meal, you can always add some of your favorite veggies like carrots in the pot to cook alongside your pork chops. You can also use ghee as a substitute for butter. If you would rather use bone-in chops, cook for 10 minutes instead of the given 5.

Cook time: 10 minutes

Serves: 5

Ingredients:

- pork chops, boneless – 4-6
- grass-fed butter – 1 stick
- ranch mix- 1 packet
- oil, coconut – 1 tablespoon
- water – 1 cup

Method:

- add your pork chops into the instant pot
- drizzle some coconut oil over the pork chops
- turn on the sauté function to allow the cops to fully brown on both sides
- gently place your butter stick on the pork chops and sprinkle the ranch mix on top
- pour the water to cover the pork and seal the instant pot
- Select Manual cooking mode, set the timer to 5 minutes
- when time is off, allow to release the pressure for another 5 minutes before taking off the lid
- Serve while hot. Enjoy!

Nutritional information: calories 244, fat 8, fiber 1, carbs 7, protein 22

Curried Coconut Chicken

When on a paleo diet, you are left with limited choices in terms of what you can eat. However, with the few options you have, you can make so many awesome dishes. Chicken is one of the ingredients which allows you to make tons of different meals, which are just as savory. The curried lemon and coconut chicken is insanely tasty, and you can add a whole bunch of veggies to make the dish more wholesome.

Cook time: 40 minutes

Serves: 6

Ingredients:

- Chicken breasts -4 lbs.
- Coconut milk, full fat – 1 can
- Curry powder – 1 tablespoon
- Turmeric – 1 teaspoon
- Salt, kosher – ½ teaspoon
- Lemon zest – 1 teaspoon

Method:

- Add the coconut milk, spices and lemon juice to a small medium bowl and mix well
- Drizzle some coconut sauce to coat the bottom of your instant pot
- Gently place your chicken in the pot
- Pour in the remaining coconut mixture over the chicken
- Cover the pot and close the valve
- Select the Poultry mode and set the timer to 15 minutes, at high pressure. For frozen chicken, add 10 more minutes
- After the timer goes off, open the valve to allow for quick release of steam

- If the chicken is still pink inside, return it into the pot and cook on a manual function, set at high pressure for an additional; 5-10 minutes
- Add the lemon zest when the chicken breasts are well done
- Served with steamed veggies and enjoy!

Nutritional information: calories 200, fat 2, fiber 1, carbs 5, protein 8

Salsa Verde Chicken

Have leftover chicken and you're not sure what to do with it? How about whipping some homemade chicken tacos? This is a quick and easy meal that requires no prior preparation, making it a perfect dinner choice. You can substitute chicken thighs for the breasts for darker meat.

Cooking time: 5 minutes

Serves: 5

Ingredients:

- Chicken breast, skinless – 1.5 lbs.
- garlic, finely minced – 1 teaspoon
- cumin – 1 teaspoon

- salsa Verde, sugar free – 1 ½ cups
- fresh cilantro, chopped – 2 tablespoons

Method:

- gently place your chicken breasts into the instant pot and season with cumin and ground garlic
- drizzle the salsa to coat the chicken
- lock the pot's lid and set to poultry mode
- once the cycle is done, allow for quick release of pressure
- Take the meat out and check if it is fully ready. Then shred using a fork
- transfer the chicken back to the pot
- stir in the cilantro
- serve and enjoy over lettuce or with tortillas and add your favorite toppings

Nutritional information: calories 200, fat 3, fiber 1, carbs 5, protein 6

Instant Coconut Quinoa

Quinoa is one of the paleo friendly cereals (or let's say pseudocereals) which you can enjoy as a side dish to your meat meals, or as a stand-alone. This is an overly simple recipe you can make in just under 30 minutes using your instant pot. It's perfect for weeknight dinners when you are tired, and have less time to spend in the kitchen. The best part? All you need are just 3 ingredients. Coconut not only brings loads of flavor to the quinoa, but also a richer consistency. Quinoa can be quite bland, hence ensure that you use more seasoning once it is cooked.

Cook time: 30 minutes

Serves: 6

Ingredients:

- Quinoa, well rinsed – 1 cup
- Coconut milk – 1 can
- Water – 1 cup
- Salt, kosher – ¼ teaspoon
- small lime, juiced and zested - 1

Method:

- add all your ingredients to the instant pot
- Select the manual mode and cook the quinoa for 5 minutes under high pressure
- allow the pot to naturally release the pressure, which can take up to 10 minutes
- fluff your quinoa using a fork
- stir in the lime zest and juice
- serve and enjoy

Nutritional Information: calories 481, fat 12, fiber 7, carbs 6, protein 17

Instant Pot Yummy Ribs

Paleo meals can just be as awesome as regular meals. For those days you want to have something different for dinner, say a Friday night, why not try these pot ribs? They are super easy to make, and so delicious. All you need is just 3 ingredients to make tender ribs that just fall off the bone. Sit back and watch these ribs become an instant hit in your family.

Cook time: 40 minutes

Serves: 5

Ingredients:

- pork ribs, baby back – 2 racks
- broth, beef – 1 cup

- barbecue sauce, sugar free
- kosher salt and black pepper

Method:

- start by slicing your ribs into thirds
- season all sides with both salt and pepper
- add the beef broth to the bottom of the instant pot
- gently place the steaming rack inside and put your seasoned pork ribs on top
- lock the pot's lid
- Select Meat mode and set the timer for 30 minutes
- once the timer beeps, opt for quick release of the pressure
- meanwhile, line your cookie sheet with aluminum foil, coated with non-stick cooking spray
- gently place your cooked ribs on the sheet and drizzle the barbecue sauce on the back side of your ribs
- transfer the sheet to the instant pot and sauté for about 3-4 minutes, using the Saute mode and ensuring not to burn the skin
- flip the ribs and rub the other side with the barbecue sauce
- broil for another 3-4 minutes. Transfer to the serving plate once ready
- serve and enjoy

Nutritional information: calories 240, fat 6, fiber 1, carbs 6, protein 16

Creamy Sweet Potato Mash

For the vegans, this is a super easy and fast paleo recipe that you will enjoy making. The mashed sweet potatoes turn out buttery smooth, creamy and with loads of texture. This also makes for an ideal thanksgiving dinner dish.

Cook time: 25 minutes

Serves: 4

Ingredients:

- garnet sweet potatoes, 1-inch chunk slices – 2 pounds
- organic butter, unsalted – 3 tablespoons
- maple syrup – 2 tablespoons
- nutmeg – ¼ teaspoon
- tap water, cold – 1 cup
- sea salt, fine

Method:

- pour the cold water into your instant pot and place a steamer basket in the pot
- gently add the sweet potato chunks into the basket
- close the lid and cook your sweet potatoes under high pressure for about 8 minutes
- turn off the instant pot and allow for a quick pressure release
- open the lid and transfer the cooked potatoes to a large mixing bowl
- using a potato masher, mash them partially as you add the nutmeg, butter and maple syrup
- keep mashing until you achieve your desired consistency
- season with a pinch of salt
- serve and enjoy

Nutritional information: calories 135, fat 4, fiber 2, carbs 6, protein 4

PALEO SNACKS IN INSTANT POT

No one says that you cannot fill up on snacks while you are on a diet. This is why the paleo diet is one of the most amazing diets we have out there.

For your snacks, opt for baked vegetables or fruits, if you are not a fan of fresh ones. The best part? You will be using an instant pot, which cuts out the part where you are stuck in the kitchen for hours. Once you get cravings especially after a light lunch, try out one of these recipes and you will not be disappointed.

Caramelized Carrots

Carrots are a great snack you can enjoy throughout the day without worrying about gaining some extra inches on your waist. Sometimes there is a need to spice up a dish, which is what I have done with this recipe. However, since we are going paleo, I ditched the brown sugar for a sweetener, which makes a better substitute.

Cook time: 8 minutes

Serves: 6

Ingredients:

- Baby carrots – 32 oz.
- water – ½ cup
- agave syrup, organic – ¼ cup

- butter, unsalted – 4 tablespoons
- sea salt – ½ teaspoon

Method:

- gently place your carrots in your instant pot
- stir in the rest of the ingredients
- cover the pot and seal to close the valve
- Select the manual cooking mode and set the timer to 4 minutes
- once done, allow for a quick release of pressure
- Toss the carrots in the sauce again and serve immediately. Enjoy!

Nutritional information: calories 100, fat 2, fiber 3, carbs 3, protein 4

Sweet Potato Snack

Sweet potatoes are a great snack option especially because they are paleo, and also, a great way to cut down on carbs. You can prepare your sweet potatoes in so many ways, but if you like your potatoes soft, try baking them in the instant pot. You will always end up in fully baked, delicious potatoes that you can enjoy with coffee or your favorite beverage.

Cook time: 10 minutes

Serves: 3

Ingredients:

- Sweet potatoes, peeled and chopped into strips or cubed – 5
- Water, cold – 1 cup

Method:

- Begin by placing the steamer rack into your instant pot
- Add cold water, followed by your chopped potatoes
- Cover the pot and turn the sealing vent to ensure its sealed
- Select the manual mode to set timer to 10 minutes
- Once the timer beeps, allow for natural release of pressure. This will take about 15 minutes
- Uncover the pot and serve. Enjoy!

Nutritional Information: calories 140, fat 2, fiber 1 carbs 2, protein 4

Baked Apples with A Twist

The great thing about apples, is that you can buy them all year long. What you will love most about this recipe, is the simplicity and similarity to oven baked apples. It's a great snack for those who wouldn't touch fresh apples. The apples may not look as perfect because they don't hold their shape, but these are creamy, delicious and overly tender. You can use any dried fruit if you don't have raisins and also substitute pumpkin pie spice for cinnamon if you're not a fan.

Cook time: 25 minutes

Serves: 6

Ingredients:

- Fresh apples, cored – 6
- Raisins – 1 oz

- Apple juice, pure -1 ½ cup
- pumpkin pie spice – 1 teaspoon

Method:

- Core the apples with a paring knife or apple corer.
- Add the raisins and pumpkin pie spice into the freed core of the apples
- Add your cored apples to the base of your instant pot
- Pour the apple juice and close the lid to fully lock in the pressure
- Select Manual cooking mode and set the manual timer at 10 minutes to cook under high pressure
- Once done, allow for natural release of pressure, which should take about 10 minutes
- Take out the apples carefully; pour the juice from instant pot on top of them. Drizzle with cinnamon. Serve and enjoy

Nutritional Information: calories 130, fat 1, fiber 2, carbs 6, protein 1

Bread Pudding

Okay, bread pudding is not entirely a paleo recipe, as we all know that bread falls into the list of foods to avoid. But opting for gluten-free sourdough bread could be an option, if you are craving for these good-old delights. In addition, this is a perfect snack especially during the fall and winter. Using an instant pot allows you preparing your pudding in the easiest way possible. You will love how tasty and filling this pudding is, making it ideal to enjoy in between meals dinner. You can enjoy the leftovers for breakfast, with warm milk and a drizzle of pure maple syrup.

Cook time: 40 minutes

Serves: 10

Ingredients:

- bread, grain free, sourdough, gluten free – 1 loaf
- coconut milk, high fat – 2 cups
- eggs – 4
- maple syrup, pure – ½ cup
- butter, melted – ½ cup
- egg yolks – 2
- vanilla extract, real – 1 tablespoon
- sea salt – ¼ teaspoon

Method:

- Start by cutting the bread into 1 inch cubes
- Select a metal bowl that will fit into your instant pot's inner stainless steel bowl and line with parchment paper
- Add your bread cubes into the bowl
- Add milk, eggs, yolks, syrup, vanilla and salt into your blender and mix for 10-15 seconds
- Without turning it off, add the butter
- Meanwhile, add 2 cups of water to your IP's inner pot and place the trivet into the IP
- Place the bowl with bread cubes on the trivet

- Drizzle your custard on the bread cubes, ensuring to coat all sides
- Using a small square parchment paper, cover the surface of the pudding preventing any pieces from sticking out
- Cover your pot and seal the vent
- Press the steam button and adjust timer to 15 minutes
- Once it's done, allow for natural release of pressure, which takes about 20 minutes then open the pot
- Allow the bowl to cool then lift up the sides of the parchment to take out the pudding
- Transfer this to a plate and flip over, such that the bottom is at the top
- Slice, serve and enjoy

Nutritional information: calories 160, fat 2, fiber 3, carbs 3, protein 4

Homemade Applesauce

Apples make for a great snack which can satisfy our sweet cravings. Making applesauce is one way you get to enjoy your apples, especially if it's the season and your orchard has loads of them. Just about everyone has an applesauce recipe, but you should consider trying making this particular one in your instant pot. For a sweeter applesauce, use a non-alcoholic cider or pure apple juice instead of the water.

Cook time: 15 minutes

Serves: 1 quart

Ingredients:

- Medium apples, cored and diced – 12
- Water – ½ cup

Method:

- Begin by placing your diced apples in the inner pot of your instant pot
- Pour in your desired liquid; water or juice
- Cut a circle piece of parchment paper to fit within the inner pot. Ensure it fully covers the apples
- Cover the pot's lid and seal the pressure valve
- Using the manual function, adjust cooking time to 10 minutes
- Once time is up, allow for natural release of pressure
- Uncover the pot and take out the parchment paper
- Use an immersion blender or a food mill to blend your sauce until smooth
- Serve and enjoy

Nutritional information: calories 57, fat 0.2, fiber 2, carbs 14, protein 0.1

PALEO DESSERTS IN INSTANT POT

What's a great meal without a delicious dessert to seal the deal? Just because you are on a diet, doesn't mean that you can't still enjoy your favorite dessert.

You may not have used an instant pot before to make dessert, but it's time you tried it out. You will be surprised at how fast, efficient and easy it is. The desserts will come out looking and tasting better than ever before.

Paleo Avocado Chocolate Cake

Did you know that with an instant pot, you can easily make your favorite cakes for desserts? The IP comes in handy when you don't have much time, since its super-fast. If you have a sweet tooth, this is your chance to try making a chocolate cake using an instant pot. You will love that it comes out super moist and fluffy, just the way you like it, in addition its fully vegan and paleo. Feel free to substitute cocoa powder for carob powder, if you don't feel like using cocoa in your paleo diet.

Cook time: 20 minutes

Serves: 5

Ingredients:

- Plantain, green – 1
- Banana, ripe – ½
- Avocado, mashed – ¼ cup

- Coconut oil, melted – 2 tablespoons
- Honey, pure – 2 tablespoons
- Carob powder (or cocoa powder) – 5 tablespoons
- Apple cider vinegar – ½ teaspoon
- Baking soda – ¾ teaspoon
- Cream of tartar- 1/8 teaspoon
- Water- 1 cup

Method:

- Add all your ingredients except for the water to a food processor and blend until you obtain a smooth texture
- Using the coconut oil, lightly grease 3 ramekins and transfer the batter about ¾ of the way
- Add the water to your instant pot and place a steaming rack into the pot
- Gently place your ramekins on the steaming rack and close the lid
- Press the manual mode and set the timer to 18 minutes under high pressure
- Once the time is up, flip the valve to allow for a quick release
- remove your ramekins from the pot, and garnish with your favorite toppings

Nutritional information: calories 243, fat 1, fiber 1, carbs 2, protein 4

Chocolate Fondue

If you have a sweet tooth, preparing and savoring this chocolate fondue will be the highlight of your meal. The great part about using an instant pot for your fondue, is that you don't really need a fondue pot. Although this recipe goes against all chocolate melting rules, try it anyway. You'll be more than impressed at the outcome.

Cook time: 11 minutes

Serves: 4

Ingredients:

- 85% Swiss chocolate, dark bittersweet – 3.5 oz.
- Coconut milk, unsweetened – 3.5 oz.
- Sweetener (optional) – 1 teaspoon
- Amaretto liquor – 1 teaspoon
- Water – 2 cups

Method:

- Add your water to your instant pot, and place a rack inside the pot
- Add the rest of your ingredients in a small ceramic heatproof container and place it into the IP
- Close the lid and ensure the valve is sealed
- Use the manual mode to set timer at 2 minutes under high pressure
- When time is up, allow for quick release of pressure and use tongs to take out the container
- Keep stirring the contents until you get a nice and smooth mixture
- Transfer this to a fondue stand with heat set at medium. If you have none, serve immediately with some fresh fruit and berries. Enjoy!

Nutritional information: calories 154, fat 7, fiber 2, carbs 15, protein 4

Tapioca Pudding

Every once in a while, it's good to spice things up in the kitchen. Ditching the regular desserts for pudding after dinner may sound good, until you realize that with most puddings, you are required to use tons of milk and sugar. Well, this tapioca pudding is totally paleo, and it's insanely tasty. It'll become an instant hit on your dinner table. If you would rather use a stainless bowl instead of the glass bowl, simply omit the water, and all ingredients to the stainless bowl.

Cook time: 20 minutes

Serves: 3

Ingredients:

- Coconut milk, full fat – 13.5 oz.
- water – 1 cup
- tapioca pearls, small – 1/3 cup
- maple syrup – ¼ cup
- vanilla extract, pure – 1 teaspoon
- sea salt – ¼ teaspoon
- nutmeg, ground – ¼ teaspoon

Method:

- pour the water into your stainless steel bowl and place it on the steaming rack in the instant pot
- add all the ingredients to an oven proof glass bowl and mix well
- place the bowl on the steaming rack and close the pot
- close the pressure valve and press on the manual button to cook for 20 minutes on low.
- once the cooking cycle is done, allow for a quick release of the pressure valve
- remove the lid and mix the tapioca dessert
- place it in the refrigerator for an hour for thickening
- Serve chilled with your favorite fresh fruits. Enjoy!

Nutritional information: calories 162, fat 4, fiber 1, carbs 3, protein 3

Blueberry Mug Cake

Looking for easy, healthy and delicious paleo dessert? This blueberry mug cake is perfect dessert after a nice lunch or dinner. Ensure that you opt for safe mugs which can handle the high pressure of an instant pot for this recipe. A great tip is spraying your jars with some non-stick cooking oil to make clean up much easier.

Cook time: 15 minutes

Serves: 1

Ingredients:

- blueberries – ½ cup
- flour, almond – 1/3 cup
- egg -1
- maple syrup – 1 tablespoon

- vanilla – ½ teaspoon
- sea salt – 1/8 teaspoon
- water – 1 cup

Method:

- add all your ingredients to a medium mixing bowl and combine well
- transfer your mixture into an 8oz mason jar or mug, taking care not to overfill since the batter rises when cooked
- place the trivet into the instant pot and add water
- cover your mug cake with aluminum foil and place into the trivet
- secure the pot's lid and close the pressure valve
- select the manual cooking mode and set timer for 10 minutes
- once done, quickly release the pressure and remove the jar using a pair of tongs
- Allow the jar to cool on a rack then serve. Enjoy!

Nutritional information: calories 148, fat 1, fiber 5.5, carbs 28, protein 6.5

Apple Chutney

There are tons of ways you can enjoy your apples. Making a healthy and sweet dessert is one way you can use the apples you just bought. If you are a fan of sweet and tart desserts, granny smith apples are your best bet. Otherwise, you can use any kind of apple for this recipe. I used collagen for the added boost of proteins, nutrients and amino acids. However, you can skip using this ingredient.

Cook time: 9 minutes

Serves: 4

Ingredients:

- Apples, cubed – 5
- Raisins – ½ cup
- Cinnamon – 1 tablespoon

- Sea salt – ½ teaspoon
- Collagen – 1 tablespoon
- Water – ¾ cups
- Coconut oil – 4 tablespoons

Method:

- Add all your ingredients into the instant pot
- Attach a rubber seal to the pot's lid and secure it
- Select the manual cooking mode and set timer to 4 minutes
- When the time is up, allow for a quick or natural release
- Serve your chutney warm or chilled. Enjoy!

Nutritional information: calories 143, fat 3, fiber 1, carbs 8, protein 3

Paleo Diet Food List

Below you will find a comprehensive list of foods allowed in paleo diet food.

Paleo diet meat and seafood.

- Poultry (chicken, turkey, duck, geese)
- Pork
- Bacon
- Ground Beef
- Grass Fed Beef
- Lamb
- Shrimp
- Lobster
- Clams
- Salmon (as well as other types of wild-caught fish)
- Rabbit
- Goat
- Eggs (duck, chicken or goose)

Paleo Diet Vegetables Paleo diet vegetables

- Asparagus
- Avocado
- Artichoke hearts
- Beets
- Brussels sprouts
- Broccoli
- Butternut Squash
- Cabbage
- Carrots
- Celery
- Cauliflower
- Eggplant
- Green Onions
- Peppers
- Parsley
- Sweet Potato
- Spinach
- Zucchini

Paleo Diet Oils/Fats Paleo diet oils.

- Avocado Oil
- Coconut oil
- Grass fed Butter
- Macadamia Oil
- Olive oil

Paleo Diet Nuts and Seeds

- Almonds
- Cashews
- Hazelnuts
- Macadamia Nut
- Pecans
- Pine Nuts
- Pumpkin Seeds
- Sunflower Seeds
- Walnuts

Paleo Diet Fruits and Berries

- Apple
- Avocado
- Bananas (in moderation)
- Blackberries
- Blueberries
- Cantaloupe
- Figs
- Grapes
- Lemon
- Lychee
- Lime
- Mango
- Oranges
- Papaya
- Peaches
- Pineapple
- Plums
- Raspberries
- Strawberries
- Tangerine

Foods Not Allowed on The Paleo Diet

Below you will find a comprehensive list of foods not allowed in paleo diet food.

Dairy

- Processed Butter
- Cheese
- Cottage Cheese
- Non fat dairy creamer
- Skim milk
- Dairy spreads
- Cream cheese
- Powdered milk
- Yogurt
- Pudding
- Frozen Yogurt
- Low fat milk
- Ice cream

Soft drinks

Candies, chocolate bars, and all other highly-processed sweets

Fruit Juices

Grains

- Bread
- Cereals
- Corn
- Muffins
- Sandwiches
- Toasts
- Wheat

Legumes

- Beans (all types of)
- Lentils
- Miso
- Peas (all types of)
- Hot Dogs
- Peanuts
- Peanut butter
- All soybean products and derivatives
- Tofu Fatty Meats
- Other low-quality meats

CONCLUSION

Thank you for purchasing and getting to the end of my book, *Instant Paleo Delight: 30 Paleo Recipes for Instant Pot.*

I believe Paleo Diet is one of the most beneficial nutritional patterns available at present since it is mostly about eating healthy and not only about losing weight. Basically it is evangelizing healthier living from healthier nutrition, and shedding weight would be among the benefits of healthier living.

If you don't own an instant pot already, it's about time you get one. You will love just how much fast and convenient it is. Moreover, you can make just about anything with its help.

I sincerely hope you enjoyed this collection of recipes, yet don't be afraid to experiment with the ingredients, within the boundaries of products allowed in Paleo diet; feel free to add and modify them to your liking and treat your loved with your culinary masterpieces.

Happy cooking!

Best Wishes,

Eric Davis

Text Copyright © Eric Davis_2018

All rights reserved. No part of this guide may be reproduced in any form without permission in writing from the publisher except in the case of brief quotations embodied in critical articles or reviews.

Legal & Disclaimer

The information contained in this book and its contents is not designed to replace or take the place of any form of medical or professional advice; and is not meant to replace the need for independent medical, financial, legal or other professional advice or services, as may be required. The content and information in this book has been provided for educational and entertainment purposes only.

The content and information contained in this book has been compiled from sources deemed reliable, and it is accurate to the best of the Author's knowledge, information and belief. However, the Author cannot guarantee its accuracy and validity and cannot be held liable for any errors and/or omissions. Further, changes are periodically made to this book as and when needed. Where appropriate and/or necessary, you must consult a professional (including but not limited to your doctor, attorney, financial advisor or such other professional advisor) before using any of the suggested remedies, techniques, or information in this book.

Upon using the contents and information contained in this book, you agree to hold harmless the Author from and against any damages, costs, and expenses, including any legal fees potentially resulting from the application of any of the information provided by this book. This disclaimer applies to any loss, damages or injury caused by the use and application, whether directly or indirectly, of any advice or information presented, whether for breach of contract, tort, negligence, personal injury, criminal intent, or under any other cause of action.

You agree to accept all risks of using the information presented inside this book.

You agree that by continuing to read this book, where appropriate and/or necessary, you shall consult a professional (including but not limited to your doctor, attorney, or financial advisor or such other advisor as needed) before using any of the suggested remedies, techniques, or information in this book.

Manufactured by Amazon.ca
Bolton, ON